3488

OPRAH WINFREY

OPRAH
WINFREY
MEDIA MOGUL

by Anne Lies

Content Consultant:
Mary McIlrath, PhD
Vice President, C&R Research

Essential Lives

CREDITS

Published by ABDO Publishing Company, 8000 West 78th Street,
Edina, Minnesota 55439. Copyright © 2011 by Abdo Consulting
Group, Inc. International copyrights reserved in all countries. No
part of this book may be reproduced in any form without written
permission from the publisher. The Essential Library™ is a
trademark and logo of ABDO Publishing Company.

Printed in the United States of America,
North Mankato, Minnesota
112010
012011

 THIS BOOK CONTAINS AT LEAST 10% RECYCLED MATERIALS.

Editor: Amy Van Zee
Copy Editor: Paula Lewis
Interior Design and Production: Kazuko Collins
Cover Design: Kazuko Collins

Library of Congress Cataloging-in-Publication Data
Lies, Anne, 1968-
  Oprah Winfrey : media mogul / by Anne Lies.
    p. cm. — (Essential lives)
  Includes bibliographical references and index.
  ISBN 978-1-61714-786-9
  1. Winfrey, Oprah—Juvenile literature. 2. Television personali-
ties—United States—Biography—Juvenile literature. 3. Actors—
United States—Biography—Juvenile literature. I. Title.
  PN1992.4.W56L48 2011
  791.4502'8092—dc22
  [B]
                                        2010037880

TABLE OF CONTENTS

Throughout her long career, Oprah has successfully ventured into television, film, and print markets.

IF AT FIRST
YOU DON'T SUCCEED . . .

*I*t was April 1, 1977, and Oprah Winfrey was about to lose her job. Only a few months earlier, the talented and ambitious young woman had been hired to report the news at WJZ-TV in Baltimore, Maryland. Even though she was only

23, Oprah was already experienced in broadcast news. She had entered the field while still in high school by reading the news for the Nashville, Tennessee, radio station WVOL. By the age of 19, she had moved on to television. She was the first African American, and the first woman, to anchor the news at Nashville's WTVF-TV.

When Oprah was hired as the coanchor of WJZ-TV's high-profile 6:00 p.m. news show in 1976, the station began a large advertising campaign to drum up interest in its newest star. Oprah's face peered down from billboards all over the city. "What's an Oprah?" the advertisements read.[1] For her part, Oprah had taken this opportunity to work in the country's tenth-largest television market though it meant that she would not be able to finish college. Pursuing her dream of becoming a television success had

A Hair-Brained Scheme

While Oprah was anchoring the news at WJZ-TV, the station executives wanted her to change her look. They sent her to what Oprah called a "chi-chi, poo-poo" salon in New York City.[2] The stylist used a special treatment on her hair and left it on too long. All of her hair fell out, and she had to wear wigs for weeks until it grew back!

been important enough to Oprah
that she had put off completing
her degree. Now, however, that all
seemed like a wasted effort.

Just the Facts

Oprah was known to be smart; she
was hardworking and had a great on-
camera personality. So why was she
sitting in her boss's office about to be
dismissed from the 6:00 p.m. news?

The station's managers were
unhappy with Oprah's work for
several reasons. One was her style of
presenting the news. Instead of just
reading the script, she often would
ad-lib, or put things in her own
words. Station executives thought
her approach was too casual. While
that might have pleased audiences
in Nashville, Baltimore viewers
were accustomed to a more formal
presentation of the news. Station
executives also were concerned that
WJZ might be losing viewers who were

What's Luck Got to Do with It?

Most people would consider Oprah Winfrey to be a very lucky woman, but she would disagree. She does not believe in good luck or bad luck. She believes that every-one is responsible for his or her own decisions, actions, achievements, and failures and that the best way to be success-ful is through hard work. It is a theme that comes up over and over again on her talk show and in the other areas of her work. "I don't believe in luck," she has said. "I think luck is preparation meeting opportunity."[3]

not used to seeing an African-American woman as a news anchor.

An even bigger problem, and one that did not seem possible for Oprah to overcome, was how emotionally involved she became with the news stories. Sometimes she would have to fight back tears as she read a sad story, and if a news item made her angry, viewers could tell that too.

Oprah knew this was a problem, not just for reading the news, but for her career as a professional journalist. A successful reporter has a strong sense of detachment, or the ability to talk about shocking or tragic events without becoming emotional. As a reporter, Oprah had a difficult time interviewing people who were grieving. She remembered,

> I would say to people at fires—and they've lost their children—"That's okay. You don't have to talk to me." Well, then [I'd] go back to the newsroom, and the news director [would say], "What do you mean they didn't have to talk to you?" I'd say, "But she just lost her child, and you know I just felt so bad."[4]

Even though Oprah did not feel like she was cut out to be a news anchor, she was crushed to have to give up her post. Since she had signed a contract with the station, she was not fired, but she was relegated to five minutes on the air at 5:30 a.m. The station managers tried to convince her she was so special that she needed to have her very own time slot, without a coanchor. Oprah was not buying it. She knew she was being demoted to a less important job. After so many successes, this failure was difficult to take. "I was devastated," she admitted, "because up until that point, I had sort of cruised."[5]

Oprah worked hard to get over her feelings of failure, but it was not easy. Not only had she been a disappointment as a newscaster, but her bosses took issue with the way she looked and talked. They insisted she change her hair and take lessons from a voice coach—they even suggested that she have plastic surgery. Oprah realized she was definitely in the wrong job and that she had better figure out what the right job was. She was interested in acting, but she knew she had to finish her contract with WJZ-TV. She decided she would just have to wait a while until something better came along.

It did not take long.

People Are Talking

WJZ-TV had a new station manager, Bill Carter, who wanted to make some changes. One of his ideas was to start a new morning talk show that would feature local stories and interviews with people from the Baltimore area. Carter wanted the new show, which would be called *People Are Talking*, to compete in the same time slot with *The Phil Donahue Show*, a very popular national talk show hosted by Phil Donahue. Carter knew it was a gamble. To be successful, *People Are Talking* would have to beat the highest-rated daytime talk show on television.

Carter wanted to give Oprah a try as a cohost for his new show. Oprah

Phil Donahue

When Oprah Winfrey began her first talk show, the Chicago-based *The Phil Donahue Show* was the highest-rated talk show in national syndication. Phil Donahue had begun the show in 1967. He credited his success to knowing what his mostly female audience wanted to see. Much of the television programming at the time assumed that women were more interested in their homes and families than in current events. In 1992, Donahue said,

> [We] got lucky, because we discovered early on that the usual idea of women's programming was a narrow, sexist view. We found that women were interested in a lot more than covered dishes and needlepoint.[6]

Donahue also pioneered a new format. At a time when talk shows consisted largely of people sitting in chairs or behind desks—not unlike on the news—he took his microphone into the audience to hear what his viewers had to say. Oprah borrowed this technique from Donahue, and it was highly effective for them both.

Many years later, Donahue compared his show with Oprah's. He said, "We are proud to have rearranged the furniture of daytime TV. We could not have known that almost 20 years later, [Oprah's] program would remodel the whole house."[7]

*Phil Donahue began his career as a radio announcer.
His television show ended in 1996.*

was not so sure. Was *People Are Talking* going to be
nothing more than a big flop? Still, she had to give
it a try.

"Like Breathing"

People Are Talking certainly was not a big flop. The
show turned out to be the perfect showcase for
Oprah's talents. Her lack of professional detachment

was not a problem. In fact, her warmth and sensitivity were a big part of her success. Oprah was good at interviewing because she was good at listening. Her friendly, easygoing personality made people feel comfortable talking to her.

After her very first interview, Oprah knew this was the right job for her. "I came off the air, thinking, 'This is what I should have been doing.' Because it was like breathing to me, like breathing."[8]

People Are Talking was a hit and so was Oprah. The show's ratings began to climb. Eventually, it became more popular with Baltimore viewers than *The Phil Donahue Show*. WJZ-TV now had the celebrity it had hoped for when Oprah was hired, and Oprah had discovered that she could be successful just being herself.

Only a year before, what had seemed like a career-ending failure was actually just the beginning of

Creating Rapport

Deborah Tannen is the author of *You Just Don't Understand: Women and Men in Conversation*. She has researched men's and women's styles of communication. According to Tannen, like most men, Donahue focused on information. Women, however, focus on creating a rapport with the people they talk to. That give-and-take style helped Oprah shine as an interviewer.

greater opportunities for Oprah Winfrey. She would eventually land her own eponymous television show, which would make her name famous worldwide. And through the launching of Harpo, her family of brands that spans television, film, print, and radio media, Oprah would touch millions of lives and change her own. ⌐

Phil Donahue and Oprah celebrated the twenty-fifth anniversary of The Phil Donahue Show *in 1992.*

Oprah with her father, Vernon Winfrey, left, and boyfriend, Stedman Graham, in 1988. Vernon provided a stable home life for young Oprah.

"THIS CHILD IS GIFTED"

I t was Easter morning in 1957, and the congregation at the Kosciusko Baptist Church was about to witness the beginning of a remarkable career. Three-year-old Oprah Winfrey, poised and polished in her best Sunday clothes, stepped forward and recited: "Jesus rose on Easter Day, Hallelujah, Hallelujah, all the angels did proclaim." In the front row, ladies fanned themselves in the warm church as they leaned toward her grandmother. "Hattie Mae," they declared, "this child is gifted."[1]

Oprah Gail Winfrey was born on January 29, 1954, in Kosciusko, Mississippi. At the time, her mother, Vernita Lee, was 19 years old. Oprah's father, Vernon Winfrey, was a soldier when he met Vernita. He was stationed at Fort Rucker—approximately 300 miles (483 km) away in Alabama. Her parents were not married. Oprah has said that she was conceived as the result of a "one day fling under an oak tree."[2] Vernon did not even know he was a father until he received a newspaper clipping from Vernita announcing Oprah's birth along with a note requesting that he send clothes for the baby girl.

At that time, rural Mississippi offered very few job opportunities for a black, single mother. Vernita followed in the footsteps of many African Americans who had relocated to northern and western states to try to escape the poverty and racial segregation of the South. She moved to Milwaukee, Wisconsin, to look for work as a housekeeper, leaving Oprah in the care of her grandparents, Hattie Mae and Earlest Lee.

LIFE ON THE FARM

It was on Hattie Mae's small farm that Oprah learned the lessons that would shape her future accomplishments. Some of the work was hard—much of the family's food was grown and raised on the farm— and Oprah had many chores. Hattie Mae owned the property, though. Despite her family's poverty, Oprah's home environment was stable. Hattie Mae was a loving but strict influence on Oprah. She believed strongly in corporal punishment, and Oprah often felt the sting of a switch for her outspoken behavior. She said,

When my grandmother used to whip my behind, she'd say, "I'm doing this because I love you." And I'd want to say, "If you loved me, you'd get that switch off my butt." I still don't think that was love.[3]

The Power of a Name

Oprah's distinctive name was not exactly planned. Her Aunt Ida chose the name "Orpah" from the Book of Ruth in the Bible, but people were confused about how to spell it, and they usually switched the *p* and the *r*. Oprah has a sense of humor about it, however. "On the birth certificate it is Orpah, but then it got translated to Oprah, so here we are. But that's great because Oprah spells Harpo backwards. I don't know what Orpah spells."[4]

Even so, as an adult, Oprah would come to appreciate her tough, old grandma.

Hattie Mae was not able to provide comforts that many people now take for granted—such as indoor plumbing or a television—but she made sure Oprah had everything she needed. She instilled in the young girl the values of faith, discipline, and the importance of an education. Using the Bible as her textbook, Hattie Mae taught Oprah to read years before it was time for her to start school. Oprah later said,

> I am where I am today because my grandmother gave me the foundation for success that I was allowed to continue to build upon. My grandmother taught me to read, and that opened the door to all kinds of possibilities for me.[5]

Life on Hattie Mae's farm also taught Oprah a lesson that might have surprised her grandmother— she would not stay in rural Mississippi. Even as a little girl, Oprah knew she would not grow up to lead a life like Hattie Mae's.

In addition to her natural talents, Oprah was a determined little girl. Because she already knew how to read, Oprah found herself bored in kindergarten. Instead of just accepting the situation, though, she took matters into her own hands. She wrote her teacher a note explaining why she did not think she belonged in kindergarten. "I wrote down all the words that I knew. I said, 'I know words,' I knew Mississippi, hippopotamus. . . . And I got marched off to the principal's office and I got put in the first grade the next day."[6]

A Legacy of Education

With help, Oprah has been able to trace her family's roots back several generations. She learned that education has been a strong theme in her family's lineage. On her mother's side, Oprah's great-great-grandparents, Pearce and Henrietta Winters, were both former slaves in Mississippi. Their daughter, Amanda, was a teacher and a member of the board of trustees of the Buffalo Rosenwald School in Attala County, Mississippi. Amanda and her first husband, Nelson Presley, had eight children, including Oprah's grandmother, Hattie Mae.

On her father's side, Oprah's great-great-grandparents, Constantine and Violet Winfrey, were also former slaves. Census records from 1870 show that Constantine, then age 35, could neither read nor write. Records show that by 1880, Constantine had learned those important skills. In 1906, he moved a little shack of a schoolhouse for black children onto his property. Constantine risked the vengeance of whites who did not believe that black people should be educated at all.

Constantine and Violet's son, Sanford, was Vernon Winfrey's grandfather. Vernon remembers his grandpa as a teacher nicknamed "Professor."

HARDSHIPS IN MILWAUKEE

When Oprah was six, she was sent to Milwaukee to be reunited with her mother. By this time, Vernita had a second daughter, Patricia. Vernita was working as a house cleaner and had plans to get married. This move was difficult for Oprah for many reasons. She had no real memory of Vernita. When she left Hattie Mae's house, she was leaving behind the only mother she had ever known. In addition, Vernita's attention was divided between two daughters, and Oprah had been accustomed to having her grandmother's love all to herself. As an adult, Oprah recalls this traumatic experience as a turning point in her life. "It was horrible. But something inside me clicked . . . now that I didn't have my grandmother any more, I knew I was gonna have to take care of myself."[7]

In Milwaukee, Oprah felt isolated and unhappy. She, Vernita, and Patricia shared one rented room in a house owned by a lady named Miss Miller. Oprah soon realized that her sister enjoyed better treatment—not only from Miss Miller, but also from Vernita—because she had lighter skin than Oprah. Using school as her refuge, Oprah continued to impress her teachers. After a year, her mother's marriage plans had fallen through, and Vernita no longer believed she was up to the challenge of raising two children. She contacted Oprah's father, Vernon, in Nashville, Tennessee, and asked him to take

Oprah. Vernon and his wife, Zelma, welcomed her. While they ran a very strict household, Oprah was happy with them.

The following summer, Oprah returned to Milwaukee for a visit, but she soon found that her mother wanted her to stay permanently. Vernita was going to marry her new boyfriend, and soon a brother, Jeffrey, joined the family. As unhappy as Vernon was about this arrangement, he had no recourse and neither did Oprah. She was back in her mother's care, and the situation would get much worse before it got better.

When she was nine years old, Oprah was raped by her 19-year-old cousin. This set up a cycle of sexual abuse by relatives and friends of her mother's that would last until Oprah was 14. As is often the case with victims of abuse, Oprah felt tremendous guilt and did not tell anyone what was happening. Confused, she was afraid no one would believe her. On one level, she knew that what these men were doing was wrong, but on another, she wanted very much to be loved. At her young age, however, she did not have the maturity to know the difference between love and abuse.

Success in School

Nonetheless, Oprah continued to work hard and excel in school. She took comfort in reading. Oprah's mother and sister criticized her for always sitting in corners and reading, but she did not let their words stop her. When she was in her teens, a teacher, Eugene Abrams, recognized her potential and enrolled her in Upward Bound. This program was designed to help students who might not otherwise get a chance to go to college. In Oprah's case, it meant a scholarship to the nearly all-white Nicolet High School in a wealthy suburb of Milwaukee. As Oprah continued to excel in her schoolwork, she also learned a great deal about the differences between life for the wealthy and for the poor.

Hard to Handle

Adolescence is often a time when young adults begin to rebel against

Call for Help

No one deserves to be abused, but unfortunately it happens. Children who are abused often try to keep it a secret. Fortunately, it is easier to find help now than it was when Oprah was a child. School counselors are good resources for help, and many state and national organizations are dedicated to helping children who are experiencing abuse. Many organizations have 24-hour hotlines and counselors waiting to help.

their parents, and Oprah was no different. Smart and strong willed, she stole money from her mother and then lied to cover up what she had done. She ran away from home and was gone for several days before turning up at the home of her pastor, who brought her home. Also, like many victims of sexual abuse, Oprah became promiscuous. She invited men over to the apartment while her mother was working.

Looking Back

As an adult, Oprah understands her mother better and knows now that Vernita did the best she could. "She was tired," Oprah said of her mother. "Her way of showing love to me was getting out and going to work every day, putting clothes on my back and having food on the table. At that time, I didn't understand it."[8]

By the time Oprah was 14, Vernita had to admit she could no longer handle her daughter. She took Oprah to a detention home for girls, planning to leave her there. Fortunately for Oprah, the facility was full. They told Vernita it would be two weeks before they would have room for her daughter, which was longer than Vernita could wait. She contacted Vernon and asked him to take Oprah back to Nashville. He agreed. Oprah was about to get the chance of her lifetime.

Oprah attended a film opening with her father, Vernon,
in Nashville in 2003.

Vernon's high expectations transformed Oprah's life. Today, Oprah donates money to schools and educational programs and serves as a role model to young girls in situations similar to hers when she was growing up.

SECOND CHANCES

In 1968, Vernon took his daughter back in, and he took control. Not long after she arrived in Nashville for the second time, Oprah admitted a painful secret to her father and Zelma: she was pregnant. She was very ashamed and had not told anyone. She admitted to her condition only when it became impossible to hide it any longer. Oprah's shame was so deep that she thought about committing suicide. "All I thought about was dying and how I could kill myself," she remembers.[1] Oprah went into premature labor. Sources differ, but Oprah delivered her baby boy in late 1968 or early 1969, and he died shortly afterward. The devastating experience was not often talked about.

At that time, it was not unusual for pregnant teenage girls to be expelled from school. If that had happened, Oprah would have faced a life very much like her own mother's. To prevent that, Vernon and Zelma were prepared to raise the baby as their own so that Oprah could continue in school. After the boy died, Vernon advised his daughter, "God has chosen to take this baby . . . I think God is giving you a second chance and, if I were you, I would use it."[2] Oprah's feelings were mixed. Even though she was sad to have lost her baby, she was also relieved. She knew she was not prepared to be a parent.

High Expectations

Oprah often credits her father with saving her life. He did it with strict discipline, by emphasizing

Keeping a Journal

After Oprah moved back to her father's house, she began keeping a journal. This is a practice she continues faithfully. Like anyone else, she uses her journal as a place to keep track of ideas, examine her thoughts, and work out fears and uncertainties. In a commencement address given at Wellesley College in 1997, Oprah advised, "Keep a daily journal of the things you are thankful for. It will keep you focused on the abundance in your life."[4]

academics, and by providing the structure she did not have while living with her mother. Vernon was a barber and owned his own shop. He and Zelma lived in a modest middle-class neighborhood and had a strong standing in their community. Vernon was a deacon in the Faith United Baptist Church as well as a member of the Nashville city council.

It was immediately clear to Oprah that her father and stepmother would not tolerate the kind of wild behavior she had gotten away with in Milwaukee. Along with high expectations, Vernon was able to provide Oprah with a foundation of support that Vernita could not. Her parents even insisted on academics outside school, including reading five books every two weeks and writing book reports. Vernon was also strict about grades. "You can't bring C's in this house," he told his strong-willed daughter, "because you are not a C student . . . you are an A student. So that's what we expect in this house."[3] On the subject of boys, her parents gave

Oprah wise advice: boys would not respect her unless she respected herself.

Oprah took her parents' expectations to heart. With the ambition and talent she already possessed, her self-confidence improved, and she began to flourish. She became an honors student at Nashville's East High School. Not surprisingly, she was drawn to speech and drama clubs. Oprah became active in student politics and was elected vice president of her class as well as president of the student council. In her senior year, she was also voted most popular girl.

In 1971, she was one of two students from Tennessee chosen to attend the White House Conference on Youth in Estes Park, Colorado. Hosted by US presidents, these meetings were held approximately once per decade. The conferences focused on the most relevant topics of its time with the aim of improving the lives of children and youth in the United States. It was a great honor for young Oprah to attend the event.

Women of Substance

In high school, Oprah was inspired by the stories of women who fought against slavery, such as Harriet Tubman and Sojourner Truth. Both women were born into slavery and escaped to freedom. Tubman was an abolitionist who freed numerous slaves using the Underground Railroad, the secret network of routes and safehouses for escaped slaves. Truth was a women's rights activist and abolitionist known for her speech "Ain't I a Woman?" that she gave in 1851 at the Women's Rights Convention in Ohio. Oprah memorized and presented the speech often.

AND THE WINNER IS . . .

Oprah was beginning to be noticed. After the White House Conference on Youth, she was interviewed by John Heidelberg from the local WVOL radio station. She made such an impression on him that months later, when WVOL was looking for a teenager to represent the station in a small, local beauty pageant, Heidelberg thought of Oprah. She agreed and entered Nashville's Miss Fire Prevention contest. She did not think of herself as particularly

The 1971 White House Conference on Youth

The White House Conference on Youth was a series of meetings hosted by US presidents between 1909 and 1971. For the 1971 conference, President Richard Nixon proposed gathering a delegation of young people from all over the country as an "honest effort to improve the Nation's understanding of the concerns and ideals of our youth."[5]

The 1971 White House Conference on Youth in Colorado included a special focus on diversity. Youth delegates were people between the ages of 14 and 24, "who had achieved some kind of leadership among their peers."[6] For this conference, two youth delegates were chosen from each state, and international delegates were also invited. At the time, 17-year-old Oprah was well known in her community, especially in black churches, and was already proving herself to be a leader as vice president of her student body. Oprah was chosen as a delegate for the April conference.

The attendees were arranged in task forces that addressed the following areas: the draft and national service; drugs; economy and employment; education; environment; foreign relations; legal rights and justice; poverty; race and minority group relations; and values, ethics, and culture.

beautiful, and as the only nonwhite girl in the contest, Oprah assumed she had no chance of winning. Because of that, she was not nervous.

When the contestants were asked what they wanted to do as a career, Oprah's response was telling. While the other girls said they wanted to be teachers and nurses, Oprah took a different approach. She had seen Barbara Walters reporting the news on *The Today Show* that morning and answered that she wanted to be a broadcast journalist. The contestants were also asked what they would do if they had a million dollars. The other girls gave predictable answers such as giving the money to the poor. Oprah answered honestly, "If I had a million dollars, I would be a spendin' fool. I'm not quite sure what I would spend it on, but I would spend, spend, spend!"[7] Oprah became the first African American to win the title of Miss Fire Prevention, and no one was more surprised than Oprah.

On the Air

When Oprah returned to WVOL to pick up her prizes—a watch and digital clock—for winning the title of Miss Fire Prevention, Heidelberg had another surprise for her. He asked if she would like to hear her voice on tape, as if she really were a broadcast radio journalist. He gave her some news material, and Oprah started to read. Heidelberg could not believe what a natural she was. The warmth and expression of her speaking style were exactly what radio broadcasts require to engage listeners.

Reading Her Life

When Oprah was in high school, she discovered African-American authors whose works had profound effects on her. The book *I Know Why the Caged Bird Sings* by Maya Angelou was especially important to Oprah. In it, Angelou tells her own story of being torn between separated parents. She also writes about being raped. Amazed that there was another person who had experienced what she had, Oprah read the book over and over. Years later, the two women became close friends.

Before she really understood what was happening, several staff members, including the station manager, were in the room listening to her read. She was hired right then, at the age of 17, to be a radio newscaster.

She was still in high school, so she worked at the station after school and on weekends. She was paid $100 per week, which was very good money for a teenager at the time. Heidelberg became Oprah's mentor, training her to use the studio equipment and showing her the ropes of radio broadcasting. Her schedule must have been grueling, but she understood that the professional experience she was gaining was worth the effort.

Barbara Walters was a successful broadcast journalist who was an inspiration to young Oprah.

The early 1970s were a time of protest in the United States as people spoke out about civil rights, the Vietnam War, and other issues.

HIGHER EDUCATION, HIGHER AMBITIONS

Oprah graduated from East High in 1971. Just a few years before, she had returned to her father's house as a troubled and deeply unhappy girl. Now she had grown into a young woman who had achieved more than she would have ever believed possible while living with her mother. Nashville is home to Tennessee State University (TSU), a large, historically African-American college. Oprah enrolled there and studied drama and speech, continuing to live at home with Vernon and Zelma instead of living on campus.

Oprah continued to work hard at her studies, but the social atmosphere at the university was not easy for her. In 1971, students on university campuses all over the country were showing their dissatisfaction with American society and government through political activism and protests. The feminist movement was seeking equal rights for women, and many young people were opposed to US involvement in the Vietnam War. It was just three years after the assassination of Dr. Martin Luther King Jr., and many of Oprah's classmates at TSU were active in efforts toward racial equality for African Americans. While she was proud of her heritage, Oprah did not relate to the racial politics on campus. She was more interested in advancing her career than in politics and protests.

Oprah continued to compete in beauty pageants, winning several titles. Her winning streak ended in the summer of 1972 when she competed for the title of Miss Black America. She did not win, but the national exposure was beneficial to her budding career in broadcasting. Combined with her work at WVOL, she caught the attention of television station executives at Nashville's WTVF-TV.

And even though she did not join in protests, they helped create a major change in the landscape of civil rights—and Oprah benefited from it. Only 16 years earlier, Rosa Parks had sparked the Montgomery, Alabama, bus boycott by refusing to give up her seat on the bus to a white man. By the time Oprah was in college, a new set of policies, called affirmative action, was changing the rules of hiring. As a result, more and better employment opportunities were opening up for minorities and women. The face of television was literally changing as broadcasters were required to hire more African Americans and women as on-air personalities.

Affirmative Action

Affirmative action policies were the result of the Civil Rights Act of 1964, which prohibited employers from discriminating on the basis of race, color, religion, gender, or national origin.

TRANSITION TO TELEVISION

The CBS affiliate in Nashville, WTVF-TV, was looking for a news anchor. After hearing Oprah read the news on WVOL, the station

was interested in having her on its newscasts. By
hiring her, the station would not only satisfy two
affirmative action hiring requirements with just one
person, but it would also be gaining a very talented
news anchor. Television is an extremely competitive
business, and people who turn down opportunities
rarely get second chances. Oprah, however, turned
this interview down—not just once, but three times.
She knew that moving to television would be an
important advancement for her career, but she was
also only a sophomore in college. She was afraid that
if she got the job, she would not be able to keep up in
her classes and might have to quit school. Her drama
professor, Dr. William Cox, offered some helpful
insight. He pointed out to Oprah that the reason
people go to college is to gain access to these kinds of
career opportunities.

Oprah knew nothing about working in television,
but she aced the interview anyway. "I decided
to pretend to be Barbara Walters," she recalled,
"because that's how I'd gotten into this in the first
place. [I] did everything I thought she would do.
And I was hired."[1]

Oprah was aware that she was not hired for her
talent alone; she was the first African-American

woman to anchor the news for WTVF-TV. Her classmates at TSU criticized her, calling her a token and accusing her of trying to be white. Oprah was insulted by the things her classmates said, but more important, she knew the statements were ridiculous. Being black was hardly something she could avoid or deny. "You look in the mirror every morning, and you are black," she said. "There is a black face in your reflection."[2]

In spite of her peers' criticism, she continued to work hard at her

Barbara Walters

Barbara Walters is a broadcast journalist who broke through gender barriers in the early 1960s, paving the way for other women in television news. At the time, she was working for the NBC network and received the nickname "The Today Girl." Her projects focused mainly on women's issues. But she soon asked to travel with First Lady Jacqueline Kennedy to India and Pakistan. This assignment helped establish Walters as a serious journalist.

Walters was a regular on NBC's *The Today Show* from 1961 to 1974 and was the show's first female cohost from 1974 to 1976. In 1976, she accepted a position at ABC. She would earn a $1 million annual salary to be the cohost of the network's evening news program. In 1979, she became a contributor to ABC's *20/20* news show and eventually became a cohost. She stepped down in 2004. In 1997, Walters launched *The View*, a show hosted by women of various generations and political perspectives.

When Walters first started in television, she had to contend with rules such as not being allowed to ask her guests questions about politics or other "unladylike" topics. She went on, however, to interview presidents, important politicians, world leaders, and celebrities. She is known for her personal style of interviewing and for getting the first interview in many important stories.

broadcasting career. At 19, she was the youngest anchor WTVF had ever hired. Viewers found her charming. After three years at the station, she earned the attention of a station in the much larger market of Baltimore.

BALTIMORE: A BUMPY ROAD

During her senior year at TSU, Oprah was faced with the choice she had feared: college or career? WJZ-TV, the ABC affiliate in Baltimore, approached her and asked her to consider becoming a coanchor of their newly expanded evening news show. She knew moving to Baltimore would be an important step for her career. She also knew it meant leaving TSU before she finished her degree and that her father and stepmother would not be happy about it. However—and perhaps most important—at age 22, she knew that it was time to leave her parents' house and be out on her own.

As Oprah soon discovered, anchoring the news at WJZ-TV was a very different job from anchoring the news in Nashville. In the year after moving to Baltimore, she was faced with her first professional failure and demoted from her news job. In what were probably the hardest years of her career, she also learned the formula for her greatest success: talking. When she began working on *People Are Talking* in 1978, Oprah knew that she had found her niche. Her ability to inspire people to open up and talk to her helped her uncover the more human and personal aspects of their stories. Over the next six years, Oprah worked hard to learn all she could about her new show format and to polish her hosting skills. And in Baltimore, Oprah met Gayle King, who would become her best friend and eventually, a partner in business.

Best Friends

Gayle King has been Oprah's best friend since they met in Baltimore in 1976. In her career, King has been a reporter and a news anchor. She also had her own syndicated talk show, *The Gayle King Show*. Even after 30 years, the two women are very close and talk daily. Oprah says of her friend, "In spite of all the things that have happened to me, we laugh every night about one thing or another. She absolutely keeps me grounded."[3]

The audience loved the new show. *People Are Talking* quickly overtook Donahue in the ratings and became the leading talk show in Baltimore. The station began to rebroadcast the show in the evenings for viewers who could not watch it in its morning time slot. The show was syndicated for several months and shown in 12 other cities. It was not as successful with viewers outside Baltimore, but the experience gave Oprah a glimpse of how a show like hers could be very profitable.

Gayle King and Oprah have remained friends
since meeting in Baltimore in the 1970s.

Oprah relaxes in her Chicago, Illinois, office in 1985.

Chicago!

*I*n 1983, Oprah made her next important move. After the success of *People Are Talking*, she was looking for a new challenge. A producer from the show, Debra DiMaio, had taken a job at WLS-TV, the ABC affiliate in Chicago. Not long afterward, DiMaio called Oprah with a tip: WLS-TV was looking for someone to host its local talk show *A.M. Chicago*. Oprah worked through the night to make an audition videotape, and DiMaio delivered it to the station manager, Dennis Swanson.

As Oprah recalls, no one in Baltimore (with the exception of her friend Gayle King) really believed she would get the Chicago job. She had her own doubts too. Chicago had a reputation for being a racially polarized city. In that context, she was not sure how well she would be received. "Everybody, with the exception of my best friend, told me it wouldn't work," she said. "They said I was black, female, and overweight."[1]

However, Swanson liked what he saw on her tape—a confident, dynamic woman who was a natural on camera. He told her he did not care about her weight or her color. He knew she had better ratings with Baltimore viewers than Phil Donahue did, and he was hoping she would bring some of her magic to WLS. "I think you have a gift," he told her. "And I'd like you to share it with this television station."[2]

Similar to the *People Are Talking* show, *A.M. Chicago* was a talk show with a local focus. It was also at the bottom of the ratings. And as with the Baltimore

show, Oprah once again competed against Phil
Donahue for ratings; only this time, it was on his
home turf. Oprah was not intimidated and had firm
goals for herself and her job:

> *I had my own little game plan for Chicago. . . . In one year*
> *I'd walk down the street and people would know who I am. In*
> *two years people would watch because they'd like me. In three*
> *years I'd gain acceptance—you know, I'd see Phil Donahue*
> *getting a pizza and I'd say, "Oh, hi, Mr. Donahue. I watch*
> *your show sometimes."*[3]

Oprah took over *A.M. Chicago* with a broadcast
on January 2, 1984. From there, she completely
overhauled the show. She focused on topics and
trends that were current and often controversial.
The show also featured a live studio audience. With
her microphone in hand, Oprah moved around
the audience, talking directly with the people. The
viewers loved it, and Oprah's "game plan" occurred a
lot faster than even she had dreamed it would.

After just one month on the air, her popularity
pulled up the ratings of *A.M. Chicago* to equal those of
The Phil Donahue Show. After three months, *A.M. Chicago*
was solidly ahead in the ratings, and WLS-TV was
thrilled. Within the year, the station expanded the

show from 30 minutes to 60 minutes
and renamed it *The Oprah Winfrey Show.*
Oprah went from a $22,000 annual
salary when she started in Baltimore
to making approximately $200,000
per year in Chicago, a figure that
would have been unimaginable to her
only a year before.

Timing Is Everything

The Oprah Winfrey Show is on at 4:00 p.m. in many cities. This programming hour is very important to television stations, since viewers at that time usually will stay on the same channel to watch the evening news.

STRATEGIC PARTNERSHIP

Oprah was making herself into a star, but it would take an important partnership to make her into the queen of daytime television. Even as Oprah was enjoying her new job and her growing success, she was smart enough to know that she could not do everything by herself. When she had questions about a contract, she sought advice from an attorney—and met the man who would eventually help her become a media magnate.

Jeffrey Jacobs was a Chicago entertainment attorney in 1984 when he met Oprah. He had a reputation for being a ruthless advocate—Oprah calls him a "piranha"—for his clients, and he and Oprah were about to become a highly successful pair.[4] He quickly became her only business confidant and eventually shut down his law practice to work exclusively as her business manager.

THE COLOR PURPLE

As Oprah's career in television soared, she came into yet another opportunity—one that she had been dreaming about since she was a child. In 1985, musician and film producer Quincy Jones visited Chicago. In his hotel room, he flipped on the television and saw *The Oprah Winfrey Show.* He was currently producing a film adaptation of the book *The Color Purple* by Alice Walker. After watching Oprah in action, he knew that he had found just the person to play the character of Sofia.

Oprah had read the book several years earlier and had been so impressed by it that she bought copies for all her friends. When she heard that Jones and director Steven Spielberg were planning to make it

Published in 1982, *The Color Purple* is the story of Celie, a poor and illiterate black woman living in Georgia in the 1930s. The book centers on the relationships between the female characters. In spite of being abused by the men in her life, Celie eventually becomes independent. She gains her sense of identity because of the close bonds she has with the women around her. The novel won the Pulitzer Prize for Fiction and the National Book Award in 1983.

Despite the critical acclaim for the book, it was heavily criticized for showing African-American men in a negative light. Many critics felt the book only served to strengthen stereotypes of black men as abusive. When the film opened in 1985, African-American men protested outside the theater in Los Angeles. But many female audience members related to the women in the film.

Oprah played the role of Sofia in the film adaptation of The Color Purple.

into a film, she was determined to be a part of it.
She said,

> I didn't know Quincy Jones or Steven Spielberg, or how on
> earth I would get in this movie. I'd never acted in my life.
> But I felt it so intensely that I had to be a part of that movie
> . . . I wanted it more than anything in the world.[5]

Landing the role might have been a dream come true for Oprah, but making the movie was a challenge for her and WLS-TV. The film's shooting schedule required her to be in Hollywood, California, and South Carolina for eight weeks. This was difficult to manage since she needed to be in Chicago to shoot five shows each week. Making the film was so important to Oprah that she decided she would break her contract and leave if the station would not give her the time off. The station was inconvenienced by the new development but unwilling to lose its highly successful show host. Through a combination of guest hosts and reruns of the show, the station was able to cover the time Oprah was gone.

As usual, her determination paid off. Even though it was her very first acting role, she earned an Academy Award nomination for best supporting actress. Though she did not win the Oscar, the film brought her to national attention and proved that her dream of being an actress was possible. She said,

Natural Actress

Oprah's instinctive understanding of people helped her in her acting efforts. She was able to put herself in the shoes of her character, Sofia. "[It] is the ultimate in understanding," she said. "What it takes to take somebody else's life, make it your own, and put it out there. . . . It's almost like getting to live somebody else's life for a while."[6]

I intend to do and have it all. I want to have a movie career, a television career, a talk-show career . . . I believe in my own possibilities and I feel I can do it all.[7]

THE NEXT STEP

With the success of *The Oprah Winfrey Show* and the national attention that Oprah received from *The Color Purple*, Jacobs advised her that it was time to syndicate her show. Jacobs worked out a deal with the syndication company King World to distribute the show nationally. Two brothers, Roger and Michael King, ran King World. They had

Syndication

Syndication is a system by which television stations can buy the rights to broadcast shows that are produced by other stations or networks. Television production can be very expensive, so rather than producing their own shows, it is often more economical for television stations to buy syndicated shows. Some syndicated shows are reruns of older series, but some, as in the case of *People Are Talking,* are in national syndication right away. That means that stations can buy the rights to show a program the first time it is broadcast.

The price a station has to pay for a syndicated program depends on how popular it is and whether or not it is a rerun. New shows cost more than reruns, and the higher the Nielsen ratings, the higher the price. The Nielsen ratings are a measurement of the number of viewers for a given television show. The number of viewers determines the amount advertisers will be willing to pay to air commercials during those shows. Stations make up for higher costs by charging advertisers more to air their commercials during the show.

Syndicators sign contracts to promote certain shows to stations all around the country. The syndicators are paid every time they "rent" a program to a station.

Oprah worked with Roger King to syndicate The Oprah Winfrey Show.

syndicated the game shows *Wheel of Fortune* and *Jeopardy!* and were looking for a new show to add to their list. Test marketing showed that Oprah had an appeal that went far beyond the Chicago market. Viewers, especially female viewers, across the country were very receptive to Oprah's style and the topics she addressed. The King brothers were confident that her show would be able to draw the ratings—and advertising money—to make them all wealthy.

With a record-breaking 138 stations signed up to air her show, *The Oprah Winfrey Show* was broadcast nationally for the first time on September 8, 1986. It went to number one in local television ratings within four weeks and was the hottest-selling show King World had ever syndicated. Jacobs had negotiated a very good deal for Oprah, who received 25 percent of the gross income from syndication. Based on the earnings for its first four months, the show was expected to earn $125 million the following year. Oprah would receive $30 million of it.

Roger Ebert

When Oprah agreed to go on a date with Roger Ebert, Pulitzer Prize-winning film critic and host of the nationally syndicated show *At the Movies with Gene Siskel and Roger Ebert*, she had no idea that he would give her more than just movie advice. Over dinner at the Hamburger Hamlet, she told him she was not sure what to do about syndicating her show. He grabbed a napkin and began to do the math. "Deal done!" she said when she showed her the bottom line.[8]

In two whirlwind years, Oprah had become a millionaire many times over. However, unlike her teenaged answer to a frivolous beauty pageant question, she was not a spending fool. In fact, with help and advice from Jacobs, she began investing some of it very wisely—in herself and her business.

Oprah appeared with actresses Carol Burnett, top right, Julie Andrews, bottom right, and Dolly Parton in 1987.

Oprah received a Daytime Emmy in 1987.

TAKING CONTROL

*P*utting her show into syndication made
Oprah rich. She began considering
other ways to make television shows and movies in
addition to her daily show. In 1986, she formed
Harpo Productions Inc. The name is "Oprah"

spelled backward. She began buying the rights to books she liked so she could make them into television shows and movies through Harpo Productions.

Oprah had redefined the daytime talk show and brought it to a national audience. As her popularity with viewers grew, so did her power with the stations that carried her show. The regular viewers of her show, or her audience demographic, were mostly women between 18 and 54 years old. Many advertisers are interested in reaching this audience demographic, and they viewed *The Oprah Winfrey Show* as a gold mine. After just a few seasons in syndication, stations were paying as much as $90,000 per week to air Oprah's show. One executive observed, "Without Oprah, you're just scrambling."[1] In 1987, Oprah won her first of many Daytime Emmy Awards from the National Academy of Television Arts and Sciences. The category was for Outstanding Talk Show Host.

Jeffrey Jacobs advised Oprah to start taking more control of her show and career. He knew that the scheduling problems she ran into with the filming of *The Color Purple* would only continue if she sought other acting opportunities through Harpo

Productions. He also understood that a celebrity host such as Oprah could be replaced if the show's producers decided it was time for a change. In October 1988, Harpo Productions became the owner and producer of *The Oprah Winfrey Show*. With that purchase, Oprah was now in control.

Harpo Studios

Owning *The Oprah Winfrey Show* gave Oprah complete control over the content of the show and the direction it would take. It also gave her more personal freedom. Instead of adhering to WLS-TV's schedule of filming one show per day, she could film two each day and have days left for other projects.

Now she needed a studio where she could film her show. While she was renting studio space from WLS-TV, Jacobs told her about a building that was for sale. The Fred Niles Studio, an old television studio, was located near downtown Chicago. At 88,000 square feet (8,175 sq m), it

Harpo Productions

In addition to *The Oprah Winfrey Show*, Harpo Productions produced numerous made-for-television movies and series. The first was the 1989 miniseries *The Women of Brewster Place*, which was based on the novel by Gloria Naylor. Other films included *The Wedding*, *There Are No Children Here*, and *Their Eyes Were Watching God*, the latter of which was based on the novel by Zora Neale Hurston. One of Oprah's hopes was to bring images of African-American lives and experiences to the screen.

filled a city block. Oprah paid $10 million to buy the building and another $10 million to renovate it. When finished, it had three television studios, offices, a film screening room, and a gym. Oprah was now the third woman, and the first African American, to own a television studio.

Weighty Topics

On the show, Oprah became known as a host who instinctively knew what interested her audiences. While the production staff encouraged her to follow a script of questions, Oprah often improvised. When interviewing actor Tom Selleck, for instance, instead of following the script

Stedman Graham

Oprah met her life partner, Stedman Graham, in 1986. He asked her out several times before she agreed. She was suspicious at first about the former basketball player. She thought he was only interested in her for her fame and money. Now it is quite clear that is not the case. Graham is chairman and CEO of S. Graham and Associates, a management and marketing consulting company. He is also the founder of AAD Education, Health, and Sports (formerly Athletes Against Drugs), which is an organization dedicated to helping youth develop leadership skills.

Over their decades together, he and Oprah have weathered media attention about their relationship. When they first began dating, the press constantly asked when they would be married. They set a date but never went through with the plan. "What I do every day is so non-traditional that it would have been difficult to try to conform to a traditional way of being," Oprah explained. "And Stedman's a pretty traditional man." She adds, "Had we gotten married, we would definitely not still be together."[2]

Oprah appeared on Saturday Night Live *in 1986.*

and asking what his favorite color was, Oprah gushed about his beautiful blue eyes. Her audience loved it!

Though she did many celebrity interviews, Oprah understood that viewers were most interested in the stories and experiences of average people. They wanted to hear about the topics faced in their own lives. Weight was a favorite subject on Oprah's show. She had struggled with her weight for years. Oprah would eat when she was under stress, and she was stressed often. She later mentioned,

I used to brag, "I don't ever get stress," I'd ask, "What is stress? What does it feel like?" The reason I didn't get stressed is, I ate my way through it. [3]

In 1988, Oprah went on a strict diet and lost 67 pounds (30 kg). That November, she revealed the secret to her success. In size 10 jeans, she pulled a wagon onstage holding 67 pounds (30 kg) of animal fat. It represented the weight she once carried on her body. She had lost weight on a liquid diet.

Most audience members were happy for her. But some of her viewers were upset. They had viewed Oprah as a hero who proved that a woman did not have to be thin to be beautiful and successful. They were disappointed by her emphasis on being skinny. Throughout her career, Oprah has continued to discuss healthy eating, exercise, and weight loss.

Sweeping the Ratings

One of the reasons Oprah waited until November to tell her audience how she had lost her weight was to take advantage of the ratings sweeps. The Nielsen Company collects rating information year-round in the

Late Graduate

When Oprah left Tennessee State University to start her career in broadcasting, she had not quite finished her bachelor's degree. In 1987, she finished her degree and earned her diploma. She also gave the commencement address that year.

Controversial County

One memorable sweeps weeks show occurred in February 1987 when Oprah took her show on the road to interview residents of Forsythe County, Georgia. African Americans had been forced out of Forsythe County in 1912 and had been banned from the county ever since. Although the ban was not official, there was a strong understanding that blacks were unwelcome.

That January, a march in the county celebrating Martin Luther King Jr.'s birthday ended in violent attacks by white supremacists. Some 20,000 people from around the nation returned a few weeks later to protest. This show in Forsythe County demonstrated Oprah's sharp instincts for finding a story that would not only inform her viewers but also draw large ratings.

56 largest cities in the United States. During four months of the year (November, February, May, and July), they also collect data from the remaining, smaller markets. These ratings determine advertising rates at the local level and are very important to local television stations. They are also important to anyone who has a show syndicated in smaller markets. To increase their ratings, television producers will put their most interesting or controversial content on during sweeps weeks.

Some believe Oprah's most controversial shows were carefully timed with sweeps weeks. She and her producers knew what made interesting television and how to maximize their audience.

Oprah revealed her svelte figure on the air in November 1988.

Oprah was one of the thousands of participants who ran in the Marine Corps Marathon in Arlington, Virginia, in 1994.

MAKING CHANGES

*I*n 1988, *The Oprah Winfrey Show* was syndicated in 198 markets. In spite of her continued success, however, Oprah's weight continued to bother her. As often happens with the rapid weight loss of liquid diets, Oprah regained

the 67 pounds (30 kg) she had lost
and more. She decided to make
another all-out effort to lose weight.
This time, she enlisted the help
of personal trainer Bob Greene.
Over the course of nine months, he
helped her lose more than 70 pounds
(32 kg) through healthy eating and
exercise. She even trained for and
ran in the Marine Corps Marathon
in 1994. Once again, she shared her
success with her viewers. After years
of ups and downs with her weight, she
showed that this time her success was
because of hard work and a desire to
be healthy—not just skinny.

Oprah also had help from Rosie
Daley, her personal chef. Daley
revamped Oprah's diet, substituting
healthy, low-fat meals in place of
the high-calorie comfort foods
Oprah favored. In 1994, Daley
published a cookbook, *In the Kitchen
with Rosie: Oprah's Favorite Recipes.* Oprah
wrote the introduction for the book

Honoring Her Heritage

Oprah is proud of the African Americans, slaves, and free people who paved the way for her success today. Of this, she said, "I understand that I carry the energy of every single person who came before me and didn't have the opportunity to do what I do. . . . I carry that with me."[1]

and interviewed Daley on the show. The audience
response was electric. The book sold more than
1 million copies in the first three weeks on the
shelves. In 1996, Oprah and Bob Greene published
Make the Connection: Ten Steps to a Better Body and a Better Life.
Oprah was expanding the ways she could connect
with her audience. At the same time, the show was
undergoing a dramatic change.

Taking Out the Trash

By the early 1990s, *The Oprah Winfrey Show*
dominated the ratings with its formula of "ordinary
people" and controversial topics. It was a recipe for
success that others, such as Jenny Jones, Ricki Lake,
Sally Jessy Raphael, Jerry Springer, and Montel
Williams, followed as well. Some shows, such as
The Jerry Springer Show, were notorious for featuring
families and people in such terrible conflict that the
guests actually fought onstage. Many viewers watched
these "shock-talk" shows. Some considered *The Oprah
Winfrey Show* to be part of the problem. This frustrated
Oprah, because she had always felt she was covering
issues that would change people's lives.

By the mid-1990s, between the growing
competition of these shows and Oprah's interest

On her show, Oprah interviewed average people as well as celebrities. Arnold Schwarzenegger and Maria Shriver visited Oprah's show in 2003.

in her own self-improvement, Oprah knew it was time to make changes to her show. "I've been guilty of doing trash TV and not even thinking it was trash," she said. "I don't want to do it anymore."[2] Rather than concentrating on stories of controversy and misery, she changed the focus of the show from problems to their solutions. She knew it was risky and that she might lose some viewers. Oprah predicted, however, that her loyal audience would follow in her quest for self-discovery and self-improvement. And they did.

Oprah's Book Club

As Oprah changed the emphasis of her show, she began including topics she considered important to living a good life. As reading had always been extremely important to her, she launched Oprah's Book Club in 1996. Oprah would select a book, announce it on her show, and give free copies to the audience. Viewers could check online to see when the book club show would be aired so they could read ahead. On the book club show, segments featured the authors and a few selected readers discussing the books as a group.

Oprah did not financially benefit from the publishers. Her book club was simply another way to reach out to her audience and to deepen their interest in her show. Several books were by African-American authors, including Toni Morrison and Maya Angelou. She hoped these selections

Book Club for Kids?

Even though Oprah does not have plans to add a kids' book club to her show, she began developing reading lists for children in August 2008. Oprah's Kids' Reading List is a mix of new and classic books for infants through age 12 and older. Titles include *My People* by Langston Hughes, *The Story of Ferdinand* by Munro Leaf, *Pippi Longstocking* by Astrid Lindgren, *The Magician's Elephant* by Kate DiCamillo, *The Great Gilly Hopkins* by Katherine Paterson, and *Number the Stars* by Lois Lowry.

Oprah brought her love of reading to her audience when she announced the start of her Book Club in 1996.

would help bridge racial gaps by encouraging her large (and mostly white) audience to read literature by black authors. The book club was a huge success, not only for Oprah's show but also for the publishing industry.

After some authors and critics questioned the literary value of Oprah's book choices, she shifted the focus of the club to classic literature during the 2003 to 2005 seasons. The book club's influence was so important, however, that in 2005 a group of 160 authors wrote to Oprah asking her to return to featuring new books. "When you stopped featuring contemporary [current] authors on your program," they wrote, "Book Club members stopped buying new fiction, and this has changed the face of American publishing."[3]

Later that year, Oprah returned to new literature with a book that turned out to be controversial. *A Million Little Pieces*, by James Frey, was supposedly a memoir—a true retelling of Frey's life experiences. In the book, he describes his drug addiction, life as a criminal, and time in rehabilitation. When it was discovered that Frey made up much of the book, it was an embarrassment for Oprah. She asked Frey and his publisher to come on the show, and when they did, she demanded to know why he lied. Frey responded,

Maya Angelou

Oprah first met Maya Angelou through the pages of her book *I Know Why the Caged Bird Sings*. Years later in Baltimore, the two women met in person—and they have been great friends ever since. Angelou is an author, a poet, an entertainer, and an activist. She has written more than 20 books. She composed the poem "On the Pulse of Morning" for Bill Clinton's 1993 presidential inauguration.

In order to get through the experience of the addiction, I thought of myself as being tougher than I was and badder than I was—and it helped me cope. When I was writing the book . . . instead of being as introspective as I should have been, I clung to that image.[4]

After Oprah pressed Frey for answers, she told him that she felt as though he had "conned us all."[5] Many critics said she was too hard on him and that her reaction showed that she was taking his dishonesty personally. Others praised Oprah for holding Frey accountable for what he had written. Even though she

Influencing Law

Oprah is focused on making positive change in the world. Looking back on her experiences of childhood sexual abuse, she felt strongly that more needed to be done to protect children from abuse.

In addition to using her show to raise awareness of abuse, she also decided to push for a new law. In April 1991, she hired attorney and former Illinois governor James Thompson to draft a plan for a national registry of child abusers. Such a list would make it easier to keep track of abusers. The Federal Bureau of Investigation (FBI) would create and maintain the list that would allow employers and schools to check into the backgrounds of anyone applying for jobs working with children.

Thompson got the support of Delaware senator Joseph Biden. In 1991, Oprah spoke before the US Senate Judiciary Committee in Washington DC. She shared her painful experience of abuse with lawmakers and asked them to pass the bill into law. It became known as the "Oprah Bill." In 1993, President Bill Clinton signed the National Child Protection Act into law.

contacted Frey later and apologized for putting him on the spot on national television, Oprah wanted her audience to know that she did not appreciate being misled.

Controversies aside, as of 2010, Oprah's Book Club had featured 63 books. Every one of the selected books became a bestseller, even books such as *Anna Karenina*, which was written by Russian author Leo Tolstoy in the late nineteenth century. Once again, Oprah proved to be a woman of great influence.

Expert Assistance

Another aspect of Oprah's new direction included enlisting the help of experts. Just as she had brought Bob Greene and Rosie Daley in to help her lose weight, Oprah brought in experts to help her viewers. On topics that ranged from personal finance to home decorating, Oprah steadily widened the circle of advisers.

One well-known expert was Dr. Phil McGraw. He was a psychologist whom Oprah hired as a courtroom adviser. In 1996, *The Oprah Winfrey Show* ran a segment on "Dangerous Food." During the show, she discussed a disorder known as mad cow disease.

The fatal disease is spread through eating infected beef. "It has just stopped me cold from eating another burger! I'm stopped!" she commented.[6] After the show aired, Texas cattle ranchers sued Oprah for damaging their business. They claimed that she had such influence with her audience that her remark had caused people to stop buying beef. McGraw helped Oprah prepare for the lawsuit. With McGraw's help, Oprah won the case. The jury found that she had not been trying to hurt the beef industry. She had only been exercising her right to free speech.

Beloved

Almost everything Oprah touches seems to turn into gold. One thing that did not was a 1998 film made from Toni Morrison's book *Beloved*. Oprah produced the film and starred as the main character, Sethe, a slave. It was a very emotional project for Oprah, and she learned a great deal about herself as a woman descended from slaves. It was critically acclaimed, but unfortunately not well attended. Income from ticket sales did not cover the cost of making the film.

McGraw became a regular guest on *The Oprah Winfrey Show*, advising viewers about relationships and life choices. Other personalities would soon join in, such as interior designer Nate Berkus. By featuring experts on her show, Oprah was helping herself and her viewers seek solutions to their questions or problems. A few of these experts would eventually host their own spin-off television shows produced by Oprah.

CONTINUING AWARDS

Working hard and following her instincts paid off. Oprah has won seven Emmys for Outstanding Talk Show Host, and *The Oprah Winfrey Show* has won nine Emmys for Outstanding Talk Show. In 1998, *Time* magazine included Oprah on its list of the most influential people of the twentieth century. Oprah also received the Lifetime Achievement Award from the National Academy of Television Arts and Sciences. After that award, she removed herself from any future Emmy consideration.

Dr. Phil McGraw launched his own television show in September 2002.

On April 17, 2001, Oprah attended a party celebrating
the one-year anniversary of her magazine.

A Media Empire

*T*he *Oprah Winfrey Show* is the most successful
talk show in television history. It reaches
an estimated 42 million viewers each week in the
United States and is watched in 144 countries. The
show is the basis for what has turned into a media

empire headed by one woman—
Oprah Winfrey.

O: The Oprah Magazine

In May 2000, Oprah began a
new chapter in the story of her career
when she launched *O: The Oprah
Magazine*. The thick, glossy publication
was a joint effort with Hearst
Magazines. It featured inspirational
articles and self-improvement
information. Through the magazine,
Oprah could reach audiences other
than television viewers—perhaps
people who did not or were unable to
watch her show.

The magazine called on Oprah's experts and
featured regular columns by Dr. Phil McGraw (who
had come to be known as Dr. Phil to his fans). Other
experts included Suze Orman, who wrote about
personal finance, and Martha Beck, a life coach.
Oprah's friend Gayle King is the magazine's editor
at large. *O* has been the most successful magazine
startup in the history of the industry with the first
issue selling 1.1 million copies. Magazines usually

The Peabody Award

In 1995, Oprah won the George Foster Peabody Award. The Peabody Award is given in recognition of excellence in radio, television, and cable. Oprah was given the award "for her extraordinary commitments and achievements, consistent with the public-minded individuals who built the broadcasting profession."[1]

take five years to become profitable. *O* made money right from the start. Before long, it had 2.5 million paid subscribers.

Branching Out in Television

In 1998, Oprah invested in the Oxygen cable television network. Aimed at female viewers, it featured a half-hour program called *Oprah After the Show*. It was a chance for audience members to ask questions in a more casual atmosphere after the main show was done taping. Eventually, Oprah sold her portion of the Oxygen network.

Harpo Productions continued to make films, including *Tuesdays with Morrie,* which is based on the best-selling book by Mitch Albom. Soon, Harpo was producing shows for some of *The Oprah Winfrey Show* personalities. In September 2002, Harpo launched the *Dr. Phil* show after the success of his weekly appearances on Oprah's program. It had the highest rating of any new syndicated show since *The Oprah Winfrey Show* and continued to rank second only to Oprah in the ratings. In 2009, Harpo launched *The Dr. Oz Show*, featuring Dr. Mehmet Oz, vice-chair and professor of surgery at Columbia University. Dr. Oz is a regular contributor to Oprah's show.

Oprah's interest was not necessarily on making her company any larger—she was already a very busy woman. She told *Fortune* magazine in 2002,

> *I don't care about being bigger, because I'm already bigger than I ever expected to be. My constant focus is on being better. . . . How can I do what I'm already doing in a more forceful way?*[2]

Another way Oprah delivered her uplifting messages was through tours and personal appearances. Her "Live Your Best Life" seminar toured four cities in 2001. Attendees paid $185 each and the tour made $1.6 million.

Internet, Broadway, and Radio

Oprah's Web site also continued to develop. Today, it is a home base on the Internet for *The Oprah Winfrey Show*, her magazine, the book club, and other projects related to Oprah Winfrey and Harpo. The site has

Famous Toilet

A person as well known as Oprah is under almost constant scrutiny. Gossip and rumors can be extremely hurtful. They can also make the media appear desperate for stories. In 1997, Oprah wrote in her journal, ". . . my Florida home is on the front page of another tabloid. More notably, my toilet is on the front page. One of the workers took pictures and sold them. You know you're famous when you're not on the cover but your toilet is."[3]

Oprah joined the cast of The Color Purple *onstage
after the show's Chicago debut in 2007.*

communities, message boards, and multimedia
workshops. People visit the site for summaries of the
shows and to read interviews, advice, and articles.
Oprah's experts are also represented on the site
and contribute regular articles and blog entries.
Oprah also contributes content to the site, including
video blogs.

In 2005, 20 years after her Oscar-nominated performance as Sophia, Oprah revisited *The Color Purple* by producing it as a Broadway play. It was nominated for numerous Tony Awards, including best musical. The actress LaChanze, who played the main character Celie, won the award for Best Performance by a Leading Actress in a Musical.

In 2006, Oprah established the Oprah and Friends satellite radio channel. Some of the programs were hosted by personalities from *The Oprah Winfrey Show* and *O: The Oprah Magazine,* including Gayle King and Maya Angelou. Eventually renamed Oprah Radio, the channel now includes the exclusive program *Oprah's Soul Series*. The show, hosted by Oprah, is devoted to topics of faith and spirituality.

THE OPRAH BRAND

Oprah has become a brand name recognized around the world. Just like Nike means shoes and BMW means cars, Oprah means a multimedia empire. Her brand consists of the values that are important to her personally, such as personal empowerment, self-improvement, and charitable giving. The Oprah brand also stands for the person behind the empire, and she is very protective of her personal life. Oprah made her name by sharing a great deal of her personal life and information.

However, anyone who works for her must sign a lifelong confidentiality agreement. They promise never to talk about her or their dealings with her companies. It is very unusual, but as Oprah points out, "You wouldn't say it's harsh if you were in the tabloids all the time."[4]

Controlling her brand is the key to Oprah's continued success. Because her audience looks to her for advice and guidance as well as

Harpo

Harpo has become a family of businesses. They are:

- Harpo Inc.: The parent company that is based in Chicago.
- Harpo Films Inc.: The company that develops and produces television and feature films and is based in Los Angeles, California.
- Harpo Radio Inc.: This company produces content for the Oprah satellite radio channel and is based in Chicago.
- Harpo Studios: Home to *The Oprah Winfrey Show,* this company is located in Chicago.
- Oprah Winfrey Operating Foundations: This organization includes the foundations that make up the core of Oprah's philanthropy. It is based in Chicago.
- The Television Development Group of Harpo Productions Inc.: This company develops projects and programs to extend beyond *The Oprah Winfrey Show* and is based in Chicago.
- The Oprah Store: A freestanding retail store for Harpo Inc., which is located in Chicago.
- OWN, The Oprah Winfrey Network: Oprah's venture in this cable television network is based in Los Angeles.

entertainment, she must be very careful to protect her credibility. If her audience does not trust her judgment, her entire brand could suffer.

Oprah's media empire is succeeding, though. In 2003, *Forbes* magazine listed Oprah as one of the world's billionaires. She was the first African-American woman to make this list of the richest people in the world.

Stepping into Politics

While Oprah is careful not to do anything to harm her brand, she is still a person who must live by her beliefs. In 2007, she officially endorsed a political candidate for the first time. She chose a senator from the state of Illinois—Barack Obama.

Oprah is no stranger to the world of politics. She has interviewed many candidates and leaders on her show, including George W. Bush before he was elected president in 2000. She was also invited to President Bill Clinton's inauguration in 1993. Still, she had never backed a candidate. Doing so could possibly turn away audience members who disagreed. In 2007, she toured Iowa, South Carolina, and New Hampshire, speaking at campaign rallies with Obama. "I've never taken this kind of risk before,"

Favorite Things

Oprah is fond of giving away things. Shopping sprees for her staff and friends are not uncommon. One of the show's recurring themes is about Oprah's "Favorite Things." During the show, Oprah shares a list of items that would make good gifts— and then gives the items on the list to everyone in the audience.

she said, "because there wasn't anyone to stand up and speak up for. . . . I know [Barack Obama] is the one."[5]

Many see Oprah as a possible political figure. Her opinions do not readily conform to one party or another. Instead, she has made certain topics into her concern, such as access to education and the rights of women worldwide. She has chosen to make her impact not through politics but through generous philanthropy and contributions to her chosen causes.

Oprah introduced Barack Obama at a New Hampshire rally in 2007.

Through the Oprah Winfrey Foundation, Oprah has given money and supplies to countless people in need.

OPRAH'S ANGELS

Philanthropy has always been important to Oprah. Even before she became one of the wealthiest people in the world, she felt called to share what she had. When she was still working in Baltimore, she interviewed a young mother and her children. The family had so little that Oprah later went back to their home and took them shopping to buy winter coats.

Education, in particular, has been a focus of Oprah's giving. In 1987, she created a fund for Tennessee State University to give out ten full scholarships. The scholarships were in her father's name because Vernon Winfrey had been such an important force in Oprah's educational success. She has also given to institutions such as Morehouse College, the Harold Washington Library, and the United Negro College Fund. In 2000, Oprah gave $10 million to A Better Chance, an organization that gives gifted minority students the opportunity to go to some of the best schools in the country. "My own success has come from a strong background in reading and learning," she said. "The greatest gift you can give is the gift of learning."[1] Oprah found ways to include her audience in her charity work. In 1997, she launched Oprah's Angel Network. It began through a campaign called the World's Largest Piggy Bank in which viewers were encouraged to donate their spare change. All in all, Oprah's audience donated more than $1 million. She matched those dollars and received donations from other friends and celebrities. In less than one year, the Angel Network had raised more than $3.5 million. The money was given out as $25,000 scholarships through the Boys and Girls Clubs of America. The Angel Network also began giving $100,000 Use Your Life Awards each week on Oprah's show. Additionally, money was used to help build schools in South Africa and other countries, provide relief after natural disasters such as Hurricane Katrina, and distribute books to children.

In May 2010, the Angel Network announced it would no longer be accepting donations. The group had raised more than $80 million since its inception.

LEADERSHIP ACADEMY

Oprah has found many opportunities for charitable work in her career. She even created the reality television series *Oprah's Big Give* where participants competed to give away her money. In 2007, she opened the Oprah Winfrey Leadership Academy for Girls in Henley-on-Klip, South Africa.

Oprah contributed more than $40 million to build the school. It sits on 52 acres (21 ha) of land

On January 2, 2007, Oprah and students from the Oprah Winfrey
Leadership Academy for Girls cut the ribbon at the school's opening.

and has everything from state-of-the-art classrooms
and computer labs to a theater, a huge library, and
even a beauty salon. It is a boarding school with
dormitories that can house up to 450 students in
grades 7 through 12. The school is meant to give
underprivileged girls who have excellent academic
and leadership skills a chance at a good education.

Oprah has been criticized for the luxury of the
school. It is expensively decorated, and the girls use
china dishes. People have questioned the wisdom
of spending money on fireplaces and tennis courts
instead of using it to help more students. They have

also questioned why Oprah is willing to build such a
school in South Africa but not in the United States.

Oprah responds to that criticism by pointing out that beautiful surroundings are important to nurturing students' learning. Girls in other countries sometimes face greater barriers to their education than American girls. "I wanted this to be a place of honor for them," said Oprah, "because these girls have never been treated with kindness."[2]

Nelson Mandela, the

former president of South Africa, puts it in broader terms,

> *This school will provide opportunities to some of our young people they could never imagine. . . . The key to any country's future is in educating its youth. Oprah is therefore not only investing in a few young individuals, but in the future of our country.*[3]

Using Her Influence

Over her years on radio and television and through her donations, Oprah has had an enormous impact on American culture. From 2004 to 2010, she has been featured in every one of *Time* magazine's lists of the 100 most influential people in the world. Some of her impact is on everyday concerns. For instance, she ran a campaign to stop people from talking on cell phones while driving. The "No Phone Zone" effort hoped to cut down on the number of

The Sweetest Gift

Of the many gifts and awards Oprah has been given, none has been sweeter than the gift of a song. In 2009, while visiting the Oprah Winfrey Leadership Academy for Girls, Oprah was treated to a performance by 63 of the girls, whom Oprah calls her daughters. The girls composed the song to thank her for everything they had been given. One girl told her, "Mum Oprah, we didn't know what to give you, so we decided to give you ourselves. This is from our hearts."

"Of course," Oprah admitted, "I cried."[4]

On November 20, 2009, Oprah announced The Oprah Winfrey Show *will end in September 2011.*

accidents caused by people being distracted behind the wheel.

Other areas of impact are much bigger—such as endorsing Barack Obama for president. In every case, however, Oprah is motivated to make the world a better place with her actions. She said,

> I believe we are all given the power to use our lives as instruments. . . . If all of us would only strive for excellence in our own backyards, we would bring that excellence to the rest of the world. Yes we would.[5]

What the Future Holds

For many of her fans, it is hard to imagine what the world would be like without *The Oprah Winfrey Show*. They were about to find out, however. After 25 years on the air, the show would end in September 2011.

There is much speculation about why Oprah had decided to end the show. Some experts suggest that Oprah's ratings suffered because of her support for Barack Obama. Others think that network television advertisers were no longer interested in Oprah's viewers, who have grown older. Oprah herself says that ending the show after 25 years feels right to her.

Though her show is ending, it is not likely that Oprah will stop working. Harpo Films had a critical success in 2009 when it promoted the film *Precious*. The film won two Oscars—one for Best Adapted Screenplay and one to Mo'Nique for Best

Supporting Actress. Without a daily taping schedule, Oprah will likely find more time to pursue projects such as this.

LAUNCHING A CABLE NETWORK

The Oprah Winfrey Show was the foundation for the television and film empire Oprah has built. Now, that empire would include an entire cable network with the launching of the Oprah Winfrey Network (OWN) on January 1, 2011. In a deal announced in 2008, Discovery Communications and Harpo Inc. planned to collaborate on the new network. The Discovery Health Channel would be converted to a 24-hour cycle of programming that expands upon the Oprah brand.

The new network would be aimed at viewers 18 to 49 years old and would premier to 80 million households. Its goal is to continue the vision of *The Oprah Winfrey Show,* which is to entertain and uplift its

Vote of Confidence

Oprah's projects are considered such a sure thing that OWN did not even have its programming lined up before it had its first advertiser. In April 2010, Procter & Gamble (a company that manufactures household products such as toothpaste, razors, and laundry detergents) paid $100 million for advertising on the network. Even without audience numbers and ratings information, the company felt confident enough to enter into a three-year agreement with OWN.

audience. For Oprah, this is hardly a new development. She said,

> *Fifteen years ago, I wrote in my journal that one day I would create a television network, as I always felt my show was just the beginning of what the future could hold. For me, the launch of OWN is the evolution of the work I've been doing on television all these years and a natural extension of my show.*[6]

Success, Oprah Style

Whatever she has accomplished, and whatever is still to come, Oprah is unlikely to stop her pursuit of success and self-improvement. She noted,

> *It's very difficult for me to even see myself as successful because I still see myself as in the process of becoming successful. To me, "successful" is getting to the point where you are absolutely comfortable with yourself. And it does not matter how many things you have acquired.*[7]

Oprah on Greatness

Even with everything Oprah has accomplished, she has some very simple rules: "Don't complain about what you don't have. Use what you've got. To do less than your best is a sin. Every single one of us has the power for greatness, because greatness is determined by service—to yourself and others."[8]

From her roots as a television news reporter and anchor to owning her own studios, magazine, and television network, Oprah Winfrey has achieved the ideals of success for many. And as her media empire continues to grow, her uplifting messages will continue to reach audiences around the world. ⌐

Oprah's influence on American culture will likely last long
after her television show has ended.

Timeline

1954

On January 29, Oprah Gail Winfrey is born in Kosciusko, Mississippi.

1960

Oprah moves to Milwaukee, Wisconsin, to live with her mother and half sister.

1968

Oprah is sent to live permanently at her father's home in Nashville, Tennessee.

1977

On April 1, Oprah is demoted from her job as WJZ-TV's evening news anchor.

1978

Oprah debuts as cohost of the morning talk show *People Are Talking* on August 14.

1984

Oprah premiers as host of *A.M. Chicago* on January 2.

1971

1973

1976

Oprah is hired as a
newscaster at WVOL
radio in Nashville.
Later that year,
she graduates
from Nashville's
East High School.

WTVF-TV in Nashville
hires Oprah as an
evening news anchor.

Oprah is hired as
a news anchor at
WJZ-TV in Baltimore,
Maryland, and meets
Gayle King.

1985

1986

1986

A.M. Chicago is
renamed *The Oprah
Winfrey Show.*

On September 8, *The
Oprah Winfrey Show*
becomes nationally
syndicated.

Oprah starts Harpo
Productions Inc.

TIMELINE

1987	1988	1988
Oprah graduates from Tennessee State University and delivers the commencement address.	Harpo Productions buys the rights to *The Oprah Winfrey Show*.	Harpo Studios is established.

1998	2000	2007
On February 26, Oprah wins the Texas cattle ranchers' lawsuit.	In May, *O: The Oprah Magazine* is launched.	Oprah opens the Oprah Winfrey Leadership Academy for Girls in South Africa.

1993	1996	1997
On December 20, the National Child Protection Act, also known as the "Oprah Bill," is signed into law.	Oprah starts Oprah's Book Club.	Oprah creates the Angel Network.

2007	2008	2010
Oprah endorses Illinois Senator Barack Obama for US president.	The Oprah Winfrey Network (OWN) is formed.	*Precious*, a film promoted by Harpo Films, wins two Academy Awards on March 7.

Essential Facts

Date of Birth

January 29, 1954

Place of Birth

Kosciusko, Mississippi

Parents

Vernita Lee and Vernon Winfrey

Education

East High School in Nashville, Tennessee

Tennessee State University in Nashville, Tennessee

Marriage

Oprah has been in a relationship with Stedman Graham since 1986.

Children

A baby boy, born in late 1968 or early 1969, who died after a few months.

CAREER HIGHLIGHTS

Oprah rose to fame as the host of *The Oprah Winfrey Show,* which is the most successful talk show in television history. In the 1980s, Harpo Productions and Harpo Studios were formed and Oprah bought the rights to her show. *O: The Oprah Magazine* was launched in 2000 with great success. And in 2008, Oprah formed a television network. Her accomplishments have made her the first African-American female billionaire.

SOCIETAL CONTRIBUTIONS

Oprah's numerous acts of philanthropy include the establishment of the Oprah Winfrey Leadership Academy for Girls in South Africa. She was an advocate for the National Child Protection Act. She also established the Angel Network, which has raised more than $80 million for various causes.

CONFLICTS

Oprah was sexually abused as a child.

Throughout her adult life, Oprah has struggled with weight issues.

Cattle ranchers in Texas sued Oprah after she made remarks on the air about mad cow disease and food safety.

QUOTE

"I believe we are all given the power to use our lives as instruments. . . . If all of us would only strive for excellence in our own backyards, we would bring that excellence to the rest of the world. Yes we would."—*Oprah Winfrey*

GLOSSARY

advocate
> A person who works on behalf of a cause, a group, or a person.

affiliate
> A television station associated with another station that is able to show the same programs at the same time.

credibility
> The quality of inspiring belief and trustworthiness.

demographic
> The characteristics of a group of people, such as age or income, used to identify markets.

demoted
> To be given a less important job or position.

endorse
> To show public support and approval for someone.

eponymous
> Named after a person who is involved in the work.

frivolous
> Unimportant or not serious.

gender
> A person's sex: male or female.

gross income
> The amount of income before money is taken out for taxes or expenses.

improvise
> To act or sing without preparation; to make up a performance on the spot.

mad cow disease
> The popular name of Bovine Spongiform Encephalopathy (BSE), which is a rare but fatal brain disease spread by eating beef from infected cows.

magnate
 A person of power or importance in a certain area.

niche
 A job or an activity that fits a person's skills and interests.

notorious
 Well-known, especially for negative reasons.

philanthropy
 Efforts to promote human welfare, such as charitable donations.

polarized
 Separated into opposing groups.

sexist
 Displaying unfair treatment based on a person's gender.

syndication
 A system by which television stations buy the rights to broadcast shows that are produced by other stations or networks.

tabloids
 Newspapers that feature material about violence, crime, and scandal.

token
 A member of a minority group who is hired only to satisfy a racial requirement or quota.

ADDITIONAL RESOURCES

SELECTED BIBLIOGRAPHY

Drexler, Kateri. *Icons of Business: An Encyclopedia of Mavericks, Movers, and Shakers*. Westport, CT: Greenwood Press, 2007. Print.

Gates Jr., Henry Louis. *Finding Oprah's Roots, Finding Your Own*. New York: Crown Publishers, 2007. Print.

Mair, George. *Oprah Winfrey: The Real Story*. Secaucus, NJ: Carol, 1994. Print.

"Oprah Winfrey, Entertainment Executive: America's Beloved Best Friend." *Achievement.org*. American Academy of Achievement, 21 Feb. 1991. Web. 23 July 2010.

Rooney, Kathleen. *Reading with Oprah: The Book Club That Changed America*. Fayetteville, AR: University of Arkansas Press, 2005. Print.

Winfrey, Oprah. *The Oprah Winfrey Show: 20th Anniversary Collection*. Paramount Home Entertainment, 2005. DVD.

FURTHER READINGS

Cooper, Ilene. *Oprah Winfrey: A Twentieth-century Life*. New York: Viking, 2007. Print.

Garson, Helen S. *Oprah Winfrey: A Biography*. Westport, CT: Greenwood Press, 2004. Print.

Paprocki, Sherry Beck. *Oprah Winfrey: Talk Show Host and Media Magnate*. New York: Chelsea House, 2006. Print.

WEB LINKS

To learn more about Oprah Winfrey, visit ABDO Publishing Company online at **www.abdopublishing.com**. Web sites about Oprah Winfrey are featured on our Book Links page. These links are routinely monitored and updated to provide the most current information available.

PLACES TO VISIT

Harpo Studios
1058 West Washington Boulevard, Chicago, IL 60607
312-591-9222
www.oprah.com/oprah_tickets.html
This is the studio complex where *The Oprah Winfrey Show* and other shows are taped.

The Oprah Store
37 North Carpenter Street, Chicago, IL 60607
312-633-2100
www.theOprahstore.com
The Oprah Store sells souvenir items, clothing, and select South African arts and crafts. It includes "Oprah's Closet," a wardrobe of items once worn or treasured by Oprah. Proceeds from some sales go to benefit Oprah's Angel Network and The Oprah Winfrey Leadership Academy Foundation.

SOURCE NOTES

Chapter 1. If at First You Don't Succeed . . .

1. George Mair. *Oprah Winfrey: The Real Story.* Secaucus, NJ: Carol, 1994. Print. 43.

2. Oprah Winfrey. "Oprah's Hair Nightmare Video." *Oprah.com.* Oprah, 29 July 2008. Web. 15 May 2010.

3. Oprah Winfrey. "Oprah Winfrey Interview, Entertainment Executive: America's Beloved Best Friend." *Achievement.org.* American Academy of Achievement, 21 Feb. 1991. Web. 19 Jan. 2010.

4. Ibid.

5. Ibid.

6. Sue Murray. "Donahue, Phil." *Museum.tv.* The Museum of Broadcast Communications, n.d. Web. 19 Jan. 2010.

7. Phil Donahue. "The 2010 Time 100: Oprah Winfrey." *Time.com.* Time, 29 Apr. 2010. Web. 15 May 2010.

8. Oprah Winfrey. "Oprah Winfrey Interview, Entertainment Executive: America's Beloved Best Friend." *Achievement.org.* American Academy of Achievement, 21 Feb. 1991. Web. 19 Jan. 2010.

Chapter 2. "This Child Is Gifted"

1. Oprah Winfrey. "Oprah Winfrey Interview, Entertainment Executive: America's Beloved Best Friend." *Achievement.org.* American Academy of Achievement, 21 Feb. 1991. Web. 19 Jan. 2010.

2. Janet Lowe. *Oprah Winfrey Speaks: Insight from the World's Most Influential Voice.* New York: John Wiley & Sons, 1998. Print. 7.

3. H. W. Brands. *Masters of Enterprise: Giants of American Business from John Jacob Astor and J. P. Morgan to Bill Gates and Oprah Winfrey.* New York: The Free Press, 1999. Print. 293.

4. Oprah Winfrey. "Oprah Winfrey Interview, Entertainment Executive: America's Beloved Best Friend." *Achievement.org.* American Academy of Achievement, 21 Feb. 1991. Web. 19 Jan. 2010.

5. Ibid.

6. Henry Louis Gates Jr. *Finding Oprah's Roots, Finding Your Own.* New York: Crown Publishers, 2007. Print. 54.

7. Ibid. 49.

8. Janet Lowe. *Oprah Winfrey Speaks: Insight from the World's Most Influential Voice*. New York: John Wiley & Sons, 1998. Print. 10.

Chapter 3. Second Chances

1. Henry Louis Gates Jr. *Finding Oprah's Roots, Finding Your Own*. New York: Crown Publishers, 2007. Print. 57.

2. Ibid. 58.

3. Oprah Winfrey. "Oprah Winfrey Interview, Entertainment Executive: America's Beloved Best Friend." *Achievement.org*. American Academy of Achievement, 21 Feb. 1991. Web. 19 Jan. 2010.

4. Janet Lowe. *Oprah Winfrey Speaks: Insight from the World's Most Influential Voice*. New York: John Wiley & Sons, 1998. Print. 170.

5. John T. Woolley and Gerhard Peters. *Presidency.ucsb.edu.* The American Presidency Project Online, 13 Apr. 1972. Web. 2 July 2010.

6. "Recommendations and Resolutions: 1971 White House Conference on Youth." *Eric.ed.gov.* U.S. Government Printing Office, 1971. *Education Resources Information Center.* Web. 15 May 2010.

7. Oprah Winfrey. "Oprah Winfrey Interview, Entertainment Executive: America's Beloved Best Friend." *Achievement.org*. American Academy of Achievement, 21 Feb. 1991. Web. 19 Jan. 2010.

Chapter 4. Higher Education, Higher Ambitions

1. Oprah Winfrey. "Oprah Winfrey Interview, Entertainment Executive: America's Beloved Best Friend." *Achievement.org*. American Academy of Achievement, 21 Feb. 1991. Web. 19 Jan. 2010.

2. Ibid.

3. Janet Lowe. *Oprah Winfrey Speaks: Insight from the World's Most Influential Voice*. New York: John Wiley & Sons, 1998. Print. 43.

Source Notes Continued

Chapter 5. Chicago!

1. George Mair. *Oprah Winfrey: The Real Story*. Secaucus, NJ: Carol, 1994. Print. 73.

2. Bob Greene and Oprah Winfrey. *Make the Connection: Ten Steps to a Better Body and a Better Life*. New York: Hyperion, 1996. Print. 6.

3. H. W. Brands. *Masters of Enterprise: Giants of American Business from John Jacob Astor and J. P. Morgan to Bill Gates and Oprah Winfrey*. New York: The Free Press, 1999. Print. 297.

4. Patricia Sellers. "The Business of Being Oprah." *Money.cnn.com*. Fortune Magazine, 1 Apr. 2002. Web. 18 Aug. 2010.

5. Oprah Winfrey. "Oprah Winfrey Interview, Entertainment Executive: America's Beloved Best Friend." *Achievement.org*. American Academy of Achievement, 21 Feb. 1991. Web. 19 Jan. 2010.

6. Ibid.

7. George Mair. *Oprah Winfrey: The Real Story*. Secaucus, NJ: Carol, 1994. Print. 94.

8. "A Date With Destiny." *Oprah.com*. The Oprah Winfrey Show, 23 Nov. 2005. Web. 19 Jan. 2010.

Chapter 6. Taking Control

1. H. W. Brands. *Masters of Enterprise: Giants of American Business from John Jacob Astor and J. P. Morgan to Bill Gates and Oprah Winfrey*. New York: The Free Press, 1999. Print. 300.

2. Oprah Winfrey. "Oprah Talks to You!" *O: The Oprah Magazine* May 2010: 254. Print.

3. Janet Lowe. *Oprah Winfrey Speaks: Insight from the World's Most Influential Voice*. New York: John Wiley & Sons, 1998. Print. 111.

Chapter 7. Making Changes

1. "The Ultimate *O* Interview: Oprah Answers All *Your* Questions." *Oprah.com*. Oprah, 15 Apr. 2010. Web. 18 Aug. 2010.

2. Janet Lowe. *Oprah Winfrey Speaks: Insight from the World's Most Influential Voice*. New York: John Wiley & Sons, 1998. Print. 150.

3. David Mehegan. "Seeing Book Sales Drop, Authors Make a Plea to Oprah." *Boston.com*. The Boston Globe, 23 Apr. 2005. Web. 15 May 2010.

4. "Oprah's Questions for James." *Oprah.com*. The Oprah
Winfrey Show, 26 Jan. 2006. Web. 2 July 2010.

5. Ibid.

6. Sam Howe Verhovek. "Talk of the Town: Burgers v. Oprah."
New York Times. New York Times, 21 Jan. 1998. Web. 18 Aug. 2010.

Chapter 8. A Media Empire

1. "Oprah Winfrey Personal Award." *Peabody Awards*. Peabody
Awards, n.d. Web. 15 May 2010.

2. Patricia Sellers. "The Business of Being Oprah."
Money.cnn.com. Fortune Magazine, 1 Apr. 2002. Web. 18 Aug. 2010.

3. Oprah Winfrey. *Journey to Beloved*. New York: Hyperion, 1998.
Print. 45.

4. Patricia Sellers. "The Business of Being Oprah."
Money.cnn.com. Fortune Magazine, 1 Apr. 2002. Web. 18 Aug. 2010.

5. Sasha Johnson and Candy Crowley. "Winfrey Tells Iowa
Crowd: Barack Obama Is 'The One.'" *CNN.com*. Cable News
Network, 8 Dec. 2007. Web. 15 May 2010.

Chapter 9. Oprah's Angels

1. "Building a Dream." *Oprah.com*. O: The Oprah Magazine, 1
Jan. 2006. Web. 15 May 2010.

2. Allison Samuels. "Oprah Goes to School." *MSNBC.com*.
Microsoft Network, 8 Jan. 2007. Web. 4 Aug. 2010.

3. "Oprah opens her dream school for poor South African
children." *Orange.mu*. Orange, 2 Jan. 2007. Web. 4 Aug. 2010.

4. Oprah Winfrey. "What I Know for Sure." *O: The Oprah
Magazine* Oct. 2009: 232. Print.

5. Janet Lowe. *Oprah Winfrey Speaks: Insight from the World's Most
Influential Voice*. New York: John Wiley & Sons, 1998. Print. 134.

6. "Oprah Winfrey Network (OWN)." *Harpocareers.com*. Harpo,
n.d. Web. 15 May 2010.

7. Oprah Winfrey. "Oprah Winfrey Interview, Entertainment
Executive: America's Beloved Best Friend." *Achievement.org*.
American Academy of Achievement, 21 Feb. 1991. Web. 19 Jan.
2010.

8. Janet Lowe. *Oprah Winfrey Speaks: Insight from the World's Most
Influential Voice*. New York: John Wiley & Sons, 1998. Print. 167.

INDEX

About the Author

Anne Lies is a writer and editor who works and lives in Minneapolis, Minnesota. Her background in education includes 12 years with the Minneapolis public schools and five years tutoring writers at Metropolitan State University in Saint Paul, Minnesota. Lies holds a BA in writing and photography from Metropolitan State University. She is an avid gardener and urban farmer. During the long Minnesota winters, she likes to knit and dream about spring.

Photo Credits

Brian Zak, Sipa Press/AP Images, cover, 3; Paul Sancya/AP Images, 6; AP Images, 12, 34, 53, 54; Time & Life Pictures/Getty Images, 15, 16; Adriane Jaeckle, Stringer/Getty Images, 25, 96 (top); Getty Images, 26, 65; Stephen Chernin/AP Images, 33; FilmMagic/Getty Images, 41, 97; Charlie Knoblock/AP Images, 42, 96 (bottom); Warner Bros./AP Images, 47; Charlie Bennet/AP Images, 50, 61, 98 (top); Alan Singer, NBCU Photo Bank/AP Images, 58; Mark Wilson/AP Images, 62; Harpo Productions, Inc., George Burns/ AP Images, 67; Evan Agostini/AP Images, 73; Mark Lennihan/ AP Images, 74; Charles Rex Arbogast/AP Images, 78, 90; Elise Amendola, File/AP Images, 83, 99; Benny Gool/AP Images, 84; Denis Farrell/AP Images, 87, 98 (bottom); Sipa/AP Images, 95